WHAT PEOPLE ARE SAYING ABOUT
THE **TABLE,** THE **OIL**, & THE **CUP**

Praying common Scriptures has been a discipline practiced by people the world over. That exercise becomes an experience when the deeper meanings of those passages are known. Psalm 23, "The Lord is my shepherd," is so familiar that sometimes its wealth of wisdom is lost. We are indebted to Joey Zamora for unearthing the hidden treasure in this much-loved Psalm. You will never read it or pray it the same way again.

—Michael Pitts
Founder, Cornerstone Church, Toledo, Ohio
Cornerstone Global Network

I am so honored to endorse this wonderful book by Joey Zamora. Joey is an exceptional man with a depth of spiritual maturity and gifting way beyond his years. Equally notable is his outstanding role as husband, father, pastor, teacher, preacher, prophet, and other qualities too numerous to mention. Joey is both a cherished friend and one of the few "heroes" I have in this life. I highly recommend the man and his insightful and inspiring book.

—Larry Randolph
Senior Pastor, Peytonsville Church,
Thompson's Station, Tennessee
Conference Speaker/Author, Living Rain Ministries

Joey Zamora's latest book, *The Table, The Oil, and The Cup*, is a must-read for everyone. He takes one of the richest chapters found in Scripture and shines a new light on it that will revolutionize your spiritual journey. Joey's ability to communicate is second to none, and he proves it once again in this extraordinary book. Grab a copy. . . . read it. . . . and apply what he shares. Get ready to be impacted!

—Chris Sonksen
Founder and Global Pastor, South Hills
Church, Carona, California
Speaker/Author/Coach

The Table, The Oil, and The Cup is truly flowing with insight that runs into each chapter. The applicable revelation empowers the reader to truly lie down in green pastures and trust God! This is a must-read for all who hunger for a deeper walk with Him.

—Ruckins McKinley D.D.
Senior Pastor, New Breed Worship
Center, Santa Ana, California

My friend, my mentor, my spiritual father, the one to whom I submit my ministry, Joey Zamora has written another book, this one impacting the way you look at Psalm 23. It is a favorite to so many, yet people don't realize the significance this set of verses has for their life. Dive into this Psalm in a new way by reading this book and open yourself up to what the Lord, your shepherd, wants to speak to you.

—Rob Sanchez
LIVG Ministries, Merced, California

To: Stephanie

Enjoy the Book!

Joey Z

THE TABLE, THE OIL & THE CUP

FRESH INSIGHTS
FROM PSALM 23

PASTOR JOEY ZAMORA

ARROWS & STONES

For foreign and subsidiary rights, contact the author.

Cover design by Aaron Huskins

Cover photo by: Ilennis Martinez

ISBN: 978-1-960678-25-6   1 2 3 4 5 6 7 8 9 10

Printed in the United States of America

CONTENTS

FOREWORD

I have known Joey Zamora all his life: I am his mom! I thank the Lord for him; my heart is full, knowing he answered the call of God. Things weren't always easy; Joey has pushed himself and us all his life. As a child, you couldn't put him in a box and conform him to religion. You couldn't confine him. From the time he was eight years old, I had a mandate to pray for him, and that prayer has never ceased. It is so exciting to see him now as a great man of God, a father, a husband, a pastor, a prophet, and an apostle. He has been fitted with the revelation of wisdom and knowledge in Christ and the light with which he sees the Scriptures is beautiful. I always heard Psalm 23 at funerals, but the Lord has unveiled a fresh word in a new way. So, as you read the book, *The Table, The Oil, and The Cup*, you will taste and see that the Lord is good. You will not be the same.

Anita Zamora
Joey's mom

INTRODUCTION

Psalm 23 is one of the most iconic chapters in the Bible. It is one of the foundational texts many of us memorized as early as our Sunday school days, along with other familiar passages such as the Lord's Prayer and the priestly blessing of Numbers 6:24-27. Sometimes, however, such profound and notable Scriptures can lose their significance. Their magnitude can be overlooked in people's hearts because they stop at memorization, check it off their list of things they "need to know," and only allow the text to unfold in its meaning.

How many sermons have you heard preached on these familiar Scriptures? Well, I am here to change that. Taking a deeper dive into Psalm 23 will change your outlook and perhaps shine light on your prophetic journey in your relationship with God and His people. My purpose in writing *The Table, The Oil, and The Cup* is to illuminate this beautiful chapter written by King David, the psalmist, and give you spiritual and practical principles to encourage, motivate and perhaps inspire you to a greater hunger for God.

As we embark on this quest, my prayer for you is that God "would open the eyes of your understanding so that you may know the hope of his calling and be able to comprehend with all the saints what are the width and the length and depth and height and that you may come to know the love of Christ which passes knowledge; and that you may be filled with all the fullness of God" (Ephesians 3:18-19).

My second greatest desire is that through this book you would understand Psalm 23 more completely and see in its powerful words how much God cares for you as your shepherd. In the pages that unfold, I hope you will begin to recognize the gift of the shepherd in your life and the power of His blessing. So, sit back, buckle your seat belt, and hold on as we allow the Chief Shepherd to lead us on to green pastures, still waters, and paths of righteousness.

May He restore our mind, our will, and our emotions, so we have the strength and power to go through the valley of the shadow of death, fearing no evil because we know that His rod and His staff will comfort us through this amazing journey. And may we experience His goodness and mercy all the days of our lives, so we can become the people who make our dwelling in the house of the Lord forever and ever.

If you are ready, let's get started!

CHAPTER 1
THE GOOD CHIEF SHEPHERD

The Lord is my shepherd . . .
—Psalm 23:1, KJV

King David wrote Psalm 23. It is considered a prose-type poem, yet it has a unique rhythm and syncopation to its lyrical form. Many of David's poems were singing prose, much like what you might hear from monks singing Gregorian chanted prayers today. It should not be surprising that Psalm 23 carries a particular rhythm and sentence form, making it an easy passage to remember. It is what is known as a Psalm of Ascent or a Psalm of Degrees, in which there is an escalating point, a climatic experience.

Here it is in its entirety for us as we begin our journey (KJV):

The Lord is my shepherd; I shall not want. He maketh me to lie down in green pastures: he leadeth me beside the still waters. He restoreth my soul: he leadeth me in the paths of righteousness for his name's sake. Yea, though I walk through the valley of the shadow of death, I will fear no evil: for thou art with me; thy rod and thy staff they comfort me. Thou preparest a table before me in the presence of mine enemies: thou anointest my head with oil; my cup runneth over. Surely goodness and mercy shall follow me all the days of my life: and I will dwell in the house of the Lord for ever.

THE GOOD SHEPHERD

David was a good shepherd, writing this Psalm in the latter part of his life. He pens it after going through life's crises of ups and downs and zigs and zags, through incredible highs and very disappointing lows. The psalmist of Israel has had the privilege of experiencing firsthand how the Chief Shepherd, God Himself, has protected and preserved and at all times defended King David in his prophetic journey. The king's personal experience has brought him to a greater understanding of God's loving character as a shepherd, and he is now sharing this revelation in a song of reflection.

David's primary goal is to help the reader see and understand that God is a good and caring God over His people, like a shepherd caring for his sheep. The psalmist of Israel, in retrospect, is also reminding us that this God we all serve is the God of us all. Still, the king emphasizes that this same God who is good and caring overall is the same God who is also interested in David himself, just like a shepherd with his individual sheep and flock. David wants to express the importance of God's character as Chief Shepherd, that no matter what life throws at you, you have a great understanding of His love and concern over all that pertains to you. Whether you are feeling good or bad, rich or poor, up or down, hungry or full, God is your Chief Shepherd and you shall not want or lack in anything.

My friend, you might be struggling right now with a crazy crisis but know the same Chief Shepherd that took care of and protected and sustained King David is the same shepherd who will bring you out of your crisis. God's got you!

THE CHIEF SHEPHERD

Ezekiel 34:23-26 says, "I will establish one shepherd over them, and he shall feed them—my servant, David. He shall feed them and be their shepherd. And I, the Lord, will be their God, and My servant David a prince among them; I, the Lord, have spoken. I will make a covenant of peace with them, and cause wild beasts to cease from the land; and they will dwell safely in the wilderness and sleep in the woods. I will make them and the places all around My hill a blessing; and I will cause showers to come down in their season; there shall be showers of blessing."

The word *one* and the word *chief* denote the same thing, which is first, the highest in rank. In other words, no entity is higher in rank or before the Chief Shepherd. David is a prophetic picture and prototype of Jesus Christ, who would eventually come and be the one Chief Shepherd. He would gather the flock, feed them, and be the One who would comfort, protect, and sustain them in the midst of their troubles. The apostle Peter encourages us in his first epistle, "Shepherd the flock of God which is among us, serving as overseers, not by compulsion but willingly, not for dishonest gain but eagerly; nor as being lords over those entrusted to you, but being examples to the flock; and when the Chief Shepherd appears, you will receive the crown of glory that does not fade away" (1 Peter 5:2-5).

We have a good God, a Chief Shepherd, responsible for us. You'll hear me say this over and over again because it's so vital that you get it into your spirit and believe what the Word of God says. I want to help change your mindset to understand His responsibility towards you and begin to walk and talk like you're taken care of. The Chief Shepherd is the bishop and shepherd of your soul!

We see two parts to this first verse: 1) "The Lord is my shepherd," and 2) "I shall not want." David may have written this, but the "I" is also you and me. We are the sheep, and the Lord is our Chief Shepherd.

So, what does it mean to have a shepherd? Why won't we be in want, and more importantly, how is that possible? Eastern shepherds constantly stayed with their sheep. They would eat and sleep with their sheep. The shepherd would always spend time with the sheep so that they knew him, and he knew them. The shepherd's responsibility was to ensure that the sheep were well-protected, sustained, and comfortable. They made the sheep lie down to rest. When the shepherd is feeling good, then the sheep are feeling good!

When he wrote Psalm 23, David had been shepherding for a while both for his earthly father and his heavenly Father as he knew what it meant to tend to his earthly father's sheep literally and to tend and protect and shepherd his heavenly Father's people (Israel). In his time and culture, David was the chief shepherd, and now the Lord is our Chief Shepherd.

This shows us that the primary job of shepherds was to be responsible. They were accountable for their flocks—their safety, welfare, and sustenance. It helps us understand some of the responsibilities of our own Chief Shepherd, who God Himself appointed before the foundations of the world. We do not just have any old shepherd. We have the man, Christ Jesus, shepherding the flock of the living God. Jesus is your Father, and he is your Chief

Shepherd. If shepherds were responsible for their flock, how much more will the Lord take care of you as Father and Shepherd?

THE IMPORTANCE OF LOCAL HOUSE SHEPHERDS

It is also vital that you understand the importance of local church shepherds; they are appointed and anointed by God as delegated authority to shepherd the flock of God. They serve as under-shepherds to the one Chief Shepherd, Jesus Christ. The Lord God holds them responsible for being able to look after the people of God and provide an environment that is safe and protected, with sustenance and provision, with shelter and spiritual food.

CONCLUSION

As we embark on chapter two, where we unveil the mystery that scarcity is a myth when it comes to our loving Chief Shepherd, know that the God we serve can do exceedingly and abundantly above anything we could ask or think according to the power that is at work in us (Ephesians 3:30). Jeremiah said it like this: "Is there anything too hard for the Lord?" The answer, my friend, is NO! The Lord is our shepherd, and we shall not want!

CHAPTER 2
LACKING NOTHING

I shall not want.
—Psalm 23:1b, KJV

You and I have a shepherd who is so good at being responsible for us that the very next section of Psalm 23 tells us that we shall not want for anything. The Hebrew word used in this passage for lack is the word "chaser," *pronounced khaw-sare.* It not only means lack but decrease.[1] So, not only will your Chief Shepherd cause you not to lack, but He will also cause you not to decrease! You, His sheep, can only increase. You have to recognize Who is taking care of you!

I don't know about you, but I can envision living without lack. If you haven't memorized Philippians 4:19, you need to: "And my God shall supply all your need according to His riches in glory by Christ Jesus." This confirms how good God is! He supplies not just some of your needs, He supplies ALL your needs. Your human nature needs to learn to trust Him; Proverbs 3:5-6 declares, "Trust in the Lord with all your heart, and lean not on your own understanding; In all your ways acknowledge Him, and He shall direct your paths."

Trust Him, for your Father, the Chief Shepherd, will never fail you. For those of you who are parents, I guarantee that there isn't anything you wouldn't do for your children. Just like an earthly father, there isn't anything God wouldn't do for you.

'MY PARENTS LOVE ME THIS MUCH!'

When my wife, Meredith, and I married, she wanted to have babies almost immediately. I tried to pacify her with a puppy and then a fish tank, but nothing satisfied her desire for a baby. To say

---

1   "2638. Chaser." *Bible Hub.* https://biblehub.com/hebrew/2638.htm. Accessed 12/20.

that she was excited when we finally found out we were pregnant is an understatement! We planned for our daughter Raquel's arrival for nine months, but nothing could have prepared me for when she was born. It felt like my heart had exploded, and I held love for the first time with my two hands. I bonded with her, and I cried tears of joy. I couldn't stop.

I remember trying to "be a man." My dad was there, and there I was crying, looking at this tiny human Meredith and I had produced. At that very moment, I thought, *My parents loved me this much!* Wow! Tears started flooding my cheeks, and I understood my father's love for the first time. A few moments later, I lost my mind when I realized my heavenly Father loves me this much. Wow! Wow! Wow!

THE PARALLEL

We had already prepared a room for our daughter. We had a crib, and we bought toys—rattles, mobiles, and more dolls than you could count. We had just about anything you could think of. Something in my heart was happening when Raquel was born, and it made me, as a dad, want to give her everything that she desired. You fuss over your children, right? You're like, "Daddy loves you. He'll protect you and give you whatever you want." It's just the heart of a dad. You want to give them everything, even though they hardly respond to you in those early weeks.

But, then! Then, they start to recognize your voice. They identify your face, and the world stops for a moment. I still remember the first time Raquel began following me around a room. It didn't matter who had her or whose arms she was in; she knew that Daddy would take her to play with the plants, open the sliding door, or play with the dog or with the cat outside. I was her one-way ticket to fun and adventure, and she always wanted to do something. She got bored quickly; she got it from me! If I wanted her to come with me, I had to motion to her our secret signal. She knew that meant Daddy was going to take her to play.

WHO'S YOUR DADDY?

There was a recognition that if Daddy was signaling, he was going to take her where she needed and wanted to go, Daddy was going to protect her, Daddy was going to give her what she wanted and needed. I say all that to point us to Proverbs 3:5-6, which reads, "Trust in the Lord with all your heart and lean not on your own understanding." The word *acknowledge* means to recognize. There has to be recognition.

The problem is that there are a whole lot of folks in the kingdom of God who still don't know who their heavenly Daddy is. Look at how the Gospel of John 3:34 records it in The Message translation:

> *The One that God sent speaks God's words. And don't think he rations out the Spirit in bits and pieces. The father loves the son extravagantly. He turned everything over to him so he could give it away—a lavish distribution of gifts. That is why whoever accepts and trusts the son gets in on everything; life complete and forever! And that is also why the person*

who avoids and distrusts the son is in the dark and doesn't
see life. All he experiences of God is darkness, and an angry
darkness at that.

Just like good parents love to lavish on their children, God longs
to do the same! My question to you is, "Who's your Daddy?"

THE LOVE OF THE FATHER

There is something about the ability to rest secure once you
recognize who is on your side. When my daughter knew who
was on her side, she could rest securely. When you recognize
that God is a good shepherd and that you will not want, the
blessing activates and nothing can stop or hinder you. Nothing
can stand between you and your heavenly Daddy, and you can
rest in that revelation.

We have a Daddy whose love does not quit. It has nothing to do
with what you can or cannot do or what you did or didn't do. You
have a God who loves you so much that John 3:16 says, "God so
loved the world that He gave His only begotten Son that whoever
believes in Him should not perish but have everlasting life." When
you get the revelation of that, you become empowered. Religion
condemns, telling people who they are not instead of who they
are. Let me tell you, you are a daughter or a son of the most high
God. You have an anointing on your life. You have an assignment
and a destiny before you. You have a blessing that no one can take
away. My friend, God loves you with an everlasting love!

A STORY OF GOD'S LOVE

In 2005, we had been pastoring for only a few years at our church. I was finishing up a sermon series on the love of God entitled "Who's your Daddy?" when a widow named Joyce came up to me and said, "Pastor, I know God loves me because you prophesied to me last month that I would have the largest harvest of cherries that I have ever had in forty years."

She went on to say that during that week, when she had released the bees to pollinate, the wind was blowing up to 60 mph, and it was too windy for them to do their job. The trees didn't get pollinated. "I know that you are a man of God and that God uses you in the gift of prophecy, and I believe you," Joyce told me. "Looking at this situation, I see my orchard hasn't been pollinated but you said it would be my best year." I got scared, thinking, *Joey, what in the world did you get yourself into?* Joyce invited me to go out and see the trees, so I agreed I would visit the next day.

When I arrived, she showed me the cherry trees and how they weren't budding—a sure sign of the failed attempt to pollinate the orchard. Her insurance agent came out and met us, letting us know he would start the process of writing up a claim for the lost cherry harvest. Immediately Joyce started pointing the finger at the agent and saying that she was a child of God and that God loved her so much. Then, pointing at me, she told him, "My pastor is a man of God and he prophesied that I would have the biggest cherry harvest in forty years!" I wanted to crawl under a rock as that insurance agent said, "Joyce, are you sure you don't want to write up a claim for a loss? I know your pastor had good intentions when he prophesied to you, but you don't have cherries on any of the trees." She looked at him with the defiance of a determined child and said, "No!" She went on, "I am loved by my Daddy in heaven, and I know who my Father is. God will give me a miracle."

I gathered about twenty people in my church who I knew could pray, and the Lord gave me a strategy. I asked the prayer team to meet me at the cherry orchard at noon the following day, and I said to bring some anointing oil: we were going to anoint every tree in the orchard, prophesy life to it, and declare it would produce the biggest harvest in forty years.

We got done the following day at about 4:00 p.m., and everybody was excited but me. I was thinking, *What in the world did I get myself into?* I heard God in a whisper that evening, and He said to me, *Your prophetic word will come to pass.* A month went by, and little old Joyce came into church one Sunday morning and said, "Can you come out to the orchard tomorrow? I want to show you a miracle."

Meredith and I couldn't believe what we saw when we got there: the trees were starting to bud! God did what the bees could not do through man's obedience, prayer, and prophecy. Radio broadcaster Paul Harvey used to say, you know the rest of the story! God gave Joyce the biggest cherry harvest in forty years, and I learned a big lesson about the love of God.

I don't know what you are struggling with right now, but know that the same God who loved Joyce and the same God who loves me, is the same loving Daddy who loves you. Remember that there is nothing you can do to make God love you. He loves you!

CONCLUSION

Moving on to green pastures and still waters, I hope you have by now a good grasp of the good Chief Shepherd and His extravagant love for you and His great flock. As we embark on chapter three, we will find out that this Chief Shepherd and His great love for His sheep leads us into His abundant peace and tranquility, where we can rest and eat without fear. So come with me on this prophetic journey as we discover more beautiful gems in King David's Psalm of reflection.

CHAPTER 3

GREEN PASTURES AND STILL WATERS

He maketh me to lie down in green pastures:
he leadeth me beside the still waters.
—Psalm 23:2, KJV

What I love about our Chief Shepherd is not only is there no lack when He is in our sphere of influence, but whenever we allow Him to govern, lead, and guide, He makes us lie down in green pastures. "Make" is a big word here. It indicates that the sheep have no choice; they will recline in meadows of green pastures, which signifies abundance and life that refreshes, renews, and replenishes. This shows us that our Chief Shepherd is so good that He forces us to lie down in green pastures near the tranquility of still waters to bring revival to His sheep.

This is a place where you can go ahead and eat and not worry about a lion, a bear, a wolf, or a snake—the four things that sheep have to worry about in the wilderness. The shepherd's responsibility was to make sure that the sheep could feast without fear, and bring them into a space or place of revival where they were refreshed, renewed, and replenished.

A FRESH LOOK AT REVIVAL

Revival is not just a time or space of God coming and manifesting Himself in miracles, signs, and wonders. It is also a time and space of refreshing, renewing, and replenishing. Revival demands a crying out. All through Scripture, we see the patriarchs crying to God and Him answering their cries. Think of the children of Israel weeping and sighing, and God hearing them and raising Moses to deliver them from their Egyptian taskmasters. Or Samson crying out to God after he slayed one thousand Philistines in the desert, where he was dying of thirst and God heard him and tore a hole in the middle of a donkey's jawbone and caused water to flow out of it. Or Elijah, who stretched himself upon a little boy who had died, and God heard his desperate cry and revived the child. Revival comes to refresh and renew and replenish you.

REVIVAL REINTRODUCES YOU TO GOD

Revival is not just a series of times or spaces of refreshing, renewing, and replenishing; it is also a series of times and spaces of reintroductions. So one of the first things God does is reintroduces us to Himself so that we can experience degrees and dimensions of His presence we have never seen before. His doing this gives us an appetite for more. Once God exposes Himself to us, He can't unexposed Himself. So when God reintroduces Himself to us, He in turn introduces you to you, because you cannot see Him differently and not see yourself differently.

You can't see God as bigger and you not be stronger, you can't see God as wiser and you not be smarter. And when you get introduced to the new you, you walk differently and talk differently, and like David, you can run toward your adversary! But please note when God does this, it is not for your excitement but for your assignment because purpose requires that you have a proper perception and insight of God so that you can have a correct perception and understanding of yourself.

GOD MAKES US LIE DOWN

So God makes us lie down in green pastures so we can be revived, refreshed, renewed, and replenished so that we get a clear understanding of the Chief Shepherd and can fulfill our purpose and destiny.

When I was a kid, my mom would drop us off at my grand-mother's when she and my dad went to work. Every day after lunch, my grandma would say, "Okay, it's time to take a nap." Oh, how I hated those words! I would always say, "Do we have to take a nap?" and she always replied, "Yes, you have to." Of course, I would challenge her: "But Grandma, why?" Her reply was always the same: "Because!" Then I would say, "Because why?" And she would say, "Because I said so!"

Just like my grandmother, who knew best what we needed, our Chief Shepherd knows best what we need. He makes us lie down in the greenest pastures of life to grasp a greater revelation of our Chief Shepherd so that, in turn, we can take hold of a greater revelation of us so that we can lean and trust and see what He has provided for us in the green pasture of peace. He leads us to still waters where we can drink the water of His covenant and be satisfied.

HE LEADS US BESIDE STILL WATERS

When I was fourteen, my youth pastor took me and his two boys camping. He told us we would hike up Mount Adams, here in Washington State. He told us after we hiked five miles of grueling terrain there would be a beautiful place where we would set up camp near a canyon and a small lake. We loaded up our huge backpacks with all our food and camping gear and started hiking and hiking and more hiking; it seemed endless, but we finally got to the campsite near the canyon and right next to the small lake filled with trout.

Oh, what a beautiful sight it was: the meadow was filled with all kinds of wildflowers of purple, pink, and yellow. Hearing the birds chirping and watching the butterflies fluttering and the fish jumping seemed like paradise. It was breathtaking, and the tough five-mile hike didn't matter because this beautiful place would be home for the next three days. We sang, ate, and talked near the fire, and when it was time to go to bed, the tranquil sounds from the fish jumping and the birds singing (along with who knows what else was out there!) just brought so much peace.

THE WATERS OF PEACE

My youth pastor led us over those five miles of difficult terrain and brought us to a peaceful meadow of beauty, where we were refreshed, renewed, and replenished. Our Chief Shepherd wants to do the same for all who are called His. He brings us to and through rough terrain into places and spaces where we feel safe and can experience His divine peace. There we can build more significant levels of trust so He can reveal more excellent dimensions of Himself to us. Only then can there be a true transformation that helps us come into the revelation of His covenant, so that we can fulfill our purpose in life.

THE IMPORTANCE OF HIS COVENANT

We see the graciousness of the shepherd when we look at the life of David. He was not only a shepherd boy before he was a king but he also took responsibility when he made a covenant with Jonathan (see 1 Samuel 20). He said, in effect, "Your battle is now my battle. Your enemy is now my enemy. Everything I have belongs to you, and everything you have belongs to me." The two men made a covenant that was sacred and holy. When Jonathan was in the middle of the battle with his father, King Saul, the day they died, David became responsible for the livelihoods of Jonathan's sons because of the covenant he had made with his friend.

One of Jonathan's sons was Mephibosheth (whose name meant "a dispeller of shame,"[2]). He lived in Lo-debar, which means "no pasture."[3] His Grandfather Saul & dad were killed in battle and David became king. When news hit the palace of the death of their deaths, Mephishobeth's nursemaid hurried to remove him from the palace. In her haste to leave, she dropped him, causing him to be crippled. He was only five years old and no longer able to walk. He needed assistance to go anywhere. In that day and age, if you couldn't support yourself, you depended on somebody to care for you. Mephibosheth would have needed a caregiver to carry him and my friends this situation was the opposite of what his name declared over him.

Because of his covenant with Jonathan, David was now responsible for Mephibosheth. However, the standard course of action for a new king taking over was to kill everyone from the previous family line so they wouldn't be a threat to the new kingdom he was establishing. Mephibosheth knew this and hid from David. He did not know about the covenant his father and David had made. David knew his responsibility, though, and because of his covenant with his friend, he took care of Mephibosheth for the rest of his life. David used Ziba, who served the household of Saul,

---

2   "4648. Mephibosheth." *Bible Hub*. https://biblehub.com/hebrew/4648.htm. Accessed 12/2020.
3   "3810. Lo-debar." *Bible Hub*. https://biblehub.com/hebrew/3810.htm. Accessed 12/2020.

to help take care of Jonathan and his household. This story shows the power of covenant. It teaches us that love covers and provides for us. God wants to feel safe and provided for also, regardless of what has brought you shame or disabled you. . You may feel that you've fallen short of the grace of God, but His covenant with you means that you will continually eat at the king's table all the days of your life, just like Mephibosheth.

This is what it means to lie down in green pastures. Mephibosheth experienced it, and so can you! He knew green pastures and abundant living, drinking from still waters, not having to worry about where his provision would come from. Not only did Mephibosheth eat at the king's table, but David restored to him the land of his father and his grandfathers, and then he called Ziba and his seven sons to take care of the land on Mephishobeth's behalf. David, his chief shepherd, set him up to prosper. David was a blessing to him because he was responsible for him.

CONCLUSION

As we have journeyed along, we have grasped the heavenly insight of how our good Chief Shepherd makes us lie down in green pastures to revive, refresh, renew, and replenish us. He leads us to still waters, where we drink from the waters of covenant that bring a greater awareness of His peace and tranquility. Now we must move on and allow Him to restore our souls and lead us on our journey into righteousness, as we will discuss in more depth form in chapter four.

CHAPTER 4
RESTORING YOUR SOUL

He restoreth my soul; He leadeth me in the paths of
righteousness for his name's sake.
—Psalm 23:3, KJV

God created you a triune person, meaning that you are a spirit, you have a soul, and you live in a body. Our soul consists of our mind, our will, and our emotions. Proverbs 23:7 says that as a man "thinks in his heart, so is he." The word here for heart is the Hebrew word that denotes soul, mind, desire, emotion, and appetite. So the verse emphasizes a way of thinking that gives appetite and passion along with emotion—whether good or bad, depending on what you are setting your mind on. In Psalm 43:5 David would say, "Why are you cast down, O my soul? And why are you disquieted within me? Hope in God; for I shall yet praise Him, the help of my countenance and my God."

Our soul is a vital key to our walk with the Lord. We must learn to discipline our souls by renewing, refreshing, and replenishing our minds. The apostle Paul said it like this in Romans 12:2, "Do not be conformed to this world, but be transformed by the renewing of your mind, that you may prove what is that good and acceptable and perfect will of God." We must constantly renovate our minds with the word of our Chief Shepherd so that we may have a clearer understanding of His good, acceptable, and perfect will for our lives.

THE RESTORED SOUL

Jesus said in John 16:7, "Nevertheless I tell you the truth. It is to your advantage that I go away; for if I do not go away, the Helper [the Holy Spirit] will not come to you; but if I depart, I will send Him to you." We have the Holy Spirit as a helper to lead us and guide us into all truth, which is His word! Our Chief Shepherd uses the Spirit and the Word to help us renew, refresh, and replenish our minds to think the way God intended us to think from the very beginning.

I have discovered that my spirit was saved when I was born again, but my soul continues to be saved every day. God is delivering me daily from what I call "stinking thinking." So, it is important to constantly renew or renovate our mind, which is how we think, with the Word of God. It is the only thing that saves! In 1 Peter 1:23, the apostle writes of our "having been born again, not of corruptible seed but incorruptible through the word of God which lives and abides forever." The Word of God is the only thing that has the power to save and heal and set free. My friend, we must always endeavor to keep the Word of God preeminent in our life so we can live healthy lives for the kingdom.

A DOWNCAST SOUL

In the passage where King David says, "he restores my soul," David uses language that every shepherd would have understood. They would also have recognized what he meant in Psalm 43:11 when he talked about his soul being "cast down."

Sheep are very barrel-chested, so much so that if they are lying down to eat and overeat, they can accidentally roll over onto their back. If they do, it is tough for them to get up again. They swing their legs in the air, bleat, cry, and moan. After a few hours on their backs, all their gas starts to collect in their stomachs. This makes their belly hard and cuts off their air, eventually suffocating them. This condition is what shepherds would call being "down-cast." King David is referring to this condition in Psalm 23 when he says, "He restores my soul . . . for His name's sake." (v.3).

When a shepherd restores a cast-down sheep, he reassures it by massaging its legs to restore circulation and gently turning the sheep over onto its side. If needed, he picks that sheep up, putting it right side up so it can quickly gain its balance. What a prophetic picture of how God wants to restore all His sheep when we fall on our backs, squeal, and cry; when we fall into condemnation, guilt, and shame, or perhaps when we have suffered loss and begin to grieve, or when offense comes knocking on the door to keep us upset or angry. We have a loving Chief Shepherd who will reassure us with His great grace and mighty right arm. He can pick us up and massage us with His hands of peace so that we can regain our spiritual equilibrium.

THE OIL AND THE WINE

Luke 10:30-35 tells the great parable of the Good Samaritan:

A certain man went down from Jerusalem to Jericho, and fell among thieves, who stripped him of his clothing, wounded him, and departed, leaving him half dead. Now by chance a certain priest came down that road. And when he saw him, he passed by on the other side. Likewise a Levite, when he arrived at the place, came and looked and passed by on the other side. But a certain Samaritan, as he journeyed, came where he was. And when he saw him, he had compassion. So he went to him and bandaged his wounds, pouring on oil and wine; and he set him on his animal, brought him to an inn, and took care of him. On the next day, when he departed, he took out two denarii, gave them to the innkeeper, and said to him, "Take care of him; and whatever more you spend, when I come again, I will repay you."

Notice he poured the oil first, then the wine. This is significant because oil is a healing agent and wine is a cleansing agent. That's important because I have found out after twenty-five years of ministry that religion is more interested in cleaning you up than healing you! Notice that the Good Samaritan pours the oil and then the wine. His primary interest is healing the wounds, not cleaning them. Though cleaning is vital to wholeness, we must first heal folks up before we clean folks up. Our Chief Shepherd is interested in healing our soul before cleaning our soul. That's the power of the oil and the wine.

Knowing we have a shepherd who can restore our soul matters because our souls can become damaged and fragmented as we go through life. We all need the oil and the wine of God's Word to bring healing and deliverance, and we need to know that we have a Chief Shepherd who can put the pieces back together.

Meredith and I have been preaching and ministering as senior pastors for quite some time, and we've distributed a lot of oil and wine to people who have been through experiences in life that left them fragmented. The oil and the wine go deep into the crevices of our hearts and minds, to those places others may not see. But God knows the depths of your soul.

God leads you beside the still waters. He restores your soul and leads you in paths of righteousness. The reason He wants you to feast, the reason He wants you to drink, is so your soul can be restored. God wants to restore, revive, and reconcile you. Proverbs 4:23 says, "Keep your heart with all diligence, for out of it spring the issues of life." You must learn to guard your heart and guard your mind. Doing this allows God to heal the fragmented parts of our soul. He will cause revelation to come to us by our understanding He is our shepherd. Not only that, but He is our savior, deliverer, baptizer and provider, our sustenance, and so much more. As we get the revelation of Jesus, the living Christ, He begins to heal our fragmented minds and soul. He puts them back together. He heals them and cleans them so we can get back on the path of righteousness, where we become an asset to the kingdom of God.

THE PATHS OF RIGHTEOUSNESS

The word *paths* in this text denotes a trench, a track, or a way; it speaks of direction, and that direction is righteousness, and righteousness is a person, indicating your identity. Our Chief Shepherd is so interested in our way of righteousness that He makes sure to mention it in this awesome Psalm.

One pastor in my life speaks of "the ways of God." I love what Psalm 103:7 says: "He made known His ways unto Moses, His acts to the children of Israel." The children of Israel knew God's acts, His power, and His miracles, but Moses knew His ways, meaning Moses knew how God was doing what He was doing! We must become like Moses, who was intrigued by how

God was doing what He was doing, not just what God was doing. This text invites us to a deeper relationship with our Chief Shepherd, where we become aware of His righteousness because His ways are righteous.

It is only when you grasp the revelation of who He is and what He did for you at the cross that you are enabled to become righteous. God wants to instill an identity inside you that you are His son or daughter and you are righteous because you are a child of God! That is your passport in the kingdom, and you are righteous, just like your Chief Shepherd. When you begin to understand that you are righteous, you will start walking with a new confidence and in a new power of identity.

THE GATE OF RIGHTEOUSNESS

Psalm 118:19-20 says, "Open to me the gates of righteousness; I will go through them, and I will praise the Lord. This is the gate of the Lord, through which the righteous shall enter."

The gate of righteousness is the one that is open to every righteous believer. Paul says in 2 Corinthians 5:21, "For He made Him who knew no sin to be sin for us, that we might become the righteousness of God in Him." The cross of Calvary made us righteous. It put us in right standing with our Chief Shepherd. Once we are healed and cleansed, He gives us a revelation of His righteousness so that we can have confidence in our prophetic journey.

It's no wonder Jesus said in Matthew 6:33, "Seek first the kingdom of God and His righteousness, and all these things shall be added to you." The importance of His righteousness is powerful; you now have access to God's very throne life because He redeemed you and righteous! The door is open, not shut. Psalm 118:24 declares, "This is the day that the Lord has made; we will rejoice and be glad in it." Why? Because the door of righteousness is open to the righteous. The cross is not the end but the beginning of this glorious life in Christ Jesus, our Chief Shepherd. So come on and allow Him to restore our souls. Let Him heal and clean our souls the way He can only do it. And then let Him lead us in the paths of righteousness where we get a fresh look at the finished work of Calvary and see our beautiful identity in Christ. And when He does it, He will do it for His name's sake.

FOR HIS NAME'S SAKE

The phrase "his name's sake" here means reputation.[4] God has a reputation to uphold! When a king was in his kingdom and saw someone not taken care of properly, it reflected poorly on him. In those days, the king chose the citizens to be part of his kingdom. Notice that the Bible says that we didn't choose Him: He chose us before the foundation of the world (see Ephesians 1:4). And just like a king who chooses his people, our Chief Shepherd chooses His sheep. He has a reputation to uphold. Anything that belongs to Him, He must protect. In John 17:12, Jesus is praying to the Father and says, "While I was with them in the world, I kept them in thy name" (KJV). We are kept and protected in the name of our Lord. The word name denotes authority and character. We

---

4   "8034. Shem." *Bible Hub*. https://biblehub.com/hebrew/8034.htm. Accessed 12/2020.

are saved, guarded, and protected by His authority and character, hallelujah!

CONCLUSION

Isaiah 48:17 says, "Thus says the Lord, your Redeemer, The Holy One of Israel: 'I am the Lord your God, Who teaches you to profit, Who leads you by the way you should go." The Lord teaches you to profit. The word *profit* here means "to ascend."[5] He teaches us to ascend! Psalm 24:3-5 says, "Who may ascend into the hill of the Lord? Or who may stand in his Holy place? He who has clean hands and a pure heart, who has not lifted up his soul to an idol, nor sworn deceitfully. He shall receive blessing from the Lord, and righteousness from the God of his salvation."

The Lord is the one who teaches us to ascend so that we may be blessed with righteousness and salvation, so no matter if we have to go through the valley of the shadow of death, we don't have to fear evil, for we know that our Chief Shepherd is with us.

---

5   "3276. Yaal." *Bible Hub*. https://biblehub.com/hebrew/3276.htm. Accessed 12/2020.

CHAPTER 5
IN THE VALLEY

*In the Valley Yea though I walk through
the valley of the shadow of death,
I will fear no evil; For you are with me. Your
rod and your staff they comfort me.*
—Psalm 23:4, KJV

T he Valley of the Shadow of Death is in the Holy Land, located south of the Jericho road leading from Jerusalem to the Dead Sea. It's a place that King David was familiar with because it was there his conflict with his son Absalom took place in 2 Samuel 15:13-15. It was also the scene of Zedekiah's battle with the Babylonians in 2 Kings 25:4. Jesus used the location to tell His famous parable of the Good Samaritan.

The valley is four and a half miles long. Its side walls are over 1,500 feet high in places and only ten or twelve feet wide at the bottom. Traveling through the valley was extremely dangerous because its ground was severely eroded by sudden violent rainstorms that caused very deep gullies. The solid footing available on solid rock is so narrow in places that sheep cannot turn around. A jagged area with many caves, dens, and curves, this ravine was an easy place for people to hide in to rob passersby. It was considered the most dangerous place in Israel, called the Road of Blood or the Valley of the Shadow. Eventually, so many people died there (including one of the Herods, his spouses, and his children), that they referred to it as the Valley of the Shadow of Death.

THE SPIRITUAL PERSPECTIVE

Even though there was an actual place called the Valley of the Shadow of Death, in Psalm 23 King David reminds us that some areas in life are narrow and very bumpy because of life's rainstorms. In Matthew 7:24-27, Jesus talks about the wise master builder who builds his house on the rock. When the rain falls, the floods come, and the winds blow, the house does not fall because its foundation is on the rock. We know that the rock is Christ, according to 1 Corinthians 10:4, and if you are founded on Christ Jesus the Rock, you can outlast any storm, devil, or calamity that challenges or confronts you. Sometimes, when you can't go around the hellacious trials or over the tempestuous adversities, you must go through your own valley of the shadow of death. (Note, we are not to build a house there and live for ten years! We are supposed to go through the valley of the shadow of death.)

FEARING NO EVIL

When King David wrote Psalm 23, many wild dogs lurked in the valley of the shadow of death, looking for prey. If a flock of sheep entered the valley with their shepherd, it was common to encounter these wild dogs on the narrow paths, where it would be hard to retreat. The shepherd would sound a warning to the sheep. Then he would take out his shepherd's rod, with which he was so skilled he could throw it at an attacking dog, knocking it into the deep washed-out gullies where it would most likely die. The sheep learned to fear no evil because they were present with their shepherd, who always protected them from harm. My friends, we also must come to trust the Chief Shepherd of our souls, so that when we find ourselves in predicaments that are less than kind or find ourselves getting harassed by demonic hosts, we know we are protected by One who has a rod and a staff that will guard us from anything hell throws at us. We are secure, knowing that He is with us at all times.

HIS ROD AND HIS STAFF

Every shepherd carried a rod and a staff. The rod would guide and lead the sheep and get them out of snares, pits, and holes. Now and then, a sheep would fall into a gully or a ditch, and the shepherd would use his staff. In those days, a staff was an extension of an arm, with a half-rounded top, so the shepherd would turn the staff upside down and snatch the sheep around the neck with the round part of the staff. Or when sheep began to fight, he would wrap his staff around the aggressor's neck and tug at it to let it know to stop. The staff was also good at redirecting the sheep. If a sheep began to wander, the staff was quickly there to bring it into order. The staff was there for the shepherd to knock off, kill, and destroy the enemy coming against the sheep.

On the other hand, the rod was also a means of correction and protection. When sheep would constantly go astray, the shepherd would leave his sheep that were flocked together to go and find the lost lamb. Then he would use the rod to break the lamb's legs and put it around his neck to correct the behavior of the little lamb so that it would not get eaten by its prey.

THE SPIRITUAL APPLICATION

Hebrews 12:6-12 says, "For whom the Lord loves He chastens, and scourges every son whom He receives. If you endure chastening, God deals with you as with sons; for what son is there whom a father does not chasten? But if you are without chastening, of which all have become partakers, then you are illegitimate and not sons. Furthermore, we have had human fathers who corrected us, and we paid them respect. Shall we not much more readily be in subjection to the Father of spirits and live? For they indeed for a few days chastened us as seemed best to them, but He for our profit, that we may be partakers of His holiness. Now no chastening seems joyful for the present, but painful; afterward, it yields the peaceable fruit of righteousness to those who have been trained by it."

We serve a loving Father who is out for our welfare and knows when to use the rod or the staff in our life to prevent any harm or to protect us from all kinds of evil.

FINDING COMFORT

The word *comfort* is the word in Hebrew that denotes "strength." "Your rod and your staff, they comfort me" (v.4). I love that the rod and staff of the great Chief Shepherd can empower us. Paul says in Ephesians 6:10, "Finally . . . be strong in the Lord and in the power of His might." We must rest assured that our heavenly shepherd is watching our every move, guiding our steps so we will not slip and fall into a pit. But if we do, we can trust that the shepherd of our souls will bring a mighty deliverance with His rod and His staff.

CONCLUSION

We have a shepherd who has both a rod and a staff—one for leading, guiding, encouraging, nourishing, and correcting, and one for protecting. We don't have to fear. We can go ahead and graze. We can go ahead and drink. We can eat in peace and safety. God is our shepherd. We shall not want or lack, for He has granted us all things that pertain to life and godliness. This is our comfort!

There is comfort in knowing that you will be guided and guarded at all times by the Chief Shepherd. Regardless of where you find yourself, on mountaintops or in a valley, know we have a loving Chief Shepherd who leads and guides us to the tabletops of gorgeous green pastures.

As we embark on chapter six, we will discover that our shepherd goes and prepares a table right in the midst of our enemies. We can rest assured that He will never leave or forsake us in times of trouble.

CHAPTER 6
AT THE TABLE

Thou preparest a table before me in the presence of mine enemies.
—Psalm 23:5, KJV

T he historical backdrop to this particular Psalm is fascinating and inspiring simultaneously because the top of the Valley of the Shadow of Death was considered by all shepherds in the region to be the best green grazing and the most luxurious pastures. The table that King David is talking about is this particular tabletop of the Valley of the Shadow of Death. It has abundant supplies of food and water.

But a shepherd knew he couldn't just randomly take his sheep there anytime he wanted. The shepherd had to before the flock and prepare the tabletops before allowing his flock to feast there. It's kind of like with my wife Meredith and daughter, Raquel, who, every year, the day before Thanksgiving, would begin preparing the turkey and the ham (and of course, we can't forget the tamales!), slaving away in the kitchen preparing for our feast.

While all the boys were watching our favorite team, the Dallas Cowboys, play football, we knew when it was getting close to the great feast because Meredith would yell, "Joey, can you please set the table." That was our cue that it was about to go down! The boys would help me set the table by carefully putting out the plates at each setting, then the silverware, the salad bowls, and the glasses. Oh, and we had to remember the napkins. Then we would put out the butter, salt, pepper, hot sauce, ketchup, and of course, the gravy! It usually looked like something out of an issue of *Better Homes & Gardens* magazine; just outright gorgeous.

The shepherd had to do something like this when he prepared the table on top of the Valley of the Shadow of Death. He had to hire someone to stay with the sheep for a couple of days while he went up and prepared the table.

While doing so he had to find the crevice of every serpent in the vicinity, where he would pour oil down the crack because it acted as a repellent to the snakes. The parallel is incredible: snakes don't like oil, just like demons don't like the anointing. There was a particular weed called the camas weed that was very dangerous for the sheep to digest. They liked the camas weed because it tasted delicious, but if consumed it would be deadly.

There is a parallel here with the Mosaic Law that "religion" wants us to digest, but which if consumed can cause us to spiritually die, because we are saved by grace through faith in Jesus Christ and not by works lest any man can boast (Ephesians 2:8). The shepherd had to find all the camas weed and uproot it to keep all the sheep safe. Then he would rip off pieces of his garment and tie them to every big bush, tree, or limb to release his scent out to all the prey in the area. He was letting every lion, every bear, every wolf, and every wild dog know that there was a Chief Shepherd among those sheep. That's what it meant for a shepherd to prepare a table in the midst of his enemies.

My friend, I'm so excited because this is what God did for us: He prepared a table for us! The table is the cross of Calvary; Colossians 2:15 says that "having disarmed principalities and powers, He made a public spectacle of them, triumphing over them in it." Through the cross we have a Chief Shepherd who has cleared the way, anointed every demon hole possible, and who has left *His scent* for every demon and devil of hell to know that He is the victorious shepherd of the ages. Knowing that, we can now, with confidence, sit at the table that He has prepared and eat in peace. As we do, we can taste and see that the Lord our Chief Shepherd is good.

CONCLUSION

Ephesians 1:3 says, "Blessed be the God and Father of our Lord Jesus Christ, who hath blessed us with all spiritual blessings in the heavenly places in Christ." I am so thankful that Jesus is the Chief Shepherd who decided to go up to the mountaintop, the tabletop, of Calvary's hill and suspend Himself between heaven and earth. There, He was willing to give up the ghost on behalf of humanity so that we could graze on green pastures and drink from still waters. He did all that so we could be at peace, all while thieves, robbers, lions, bears, wolves, and serpents are trying to devour us. We have a shepherd who understands what we are going through—our temptations, our weaknesses, and the discouragement we face. This is the God we serve, and He has prepared a table for us! And God has prepared this table right in the midst of your enemies, a place where they have to watch you eat.

In Psalm 121:1, David said, "I will lift up my eyes to the hills—from whence comes my help?" Why the hills? Because when you look toward the hills, you gain a different perspective. We flew once from Las Vegas to Seattle and passed Mount Rainier:

I couldn't stop gazing at this majestic mountain. Picture David standing in the middle of a valley, during a difficult situation, in the middle of lonely and difficult places. He looked up from his circumstances to where heaven and earth meet. When you gaze at the highest place on earth, you're looking at the lowest place of the heavens—and it's a mountaintop. When you stare at that place where heaven and earth merge, you can find strength, stability, calmness, and peace.

In the next chapter, I will focus on the oil the shepherd uses and what that means for us. Are you ready?

CHAPTER 7
ANOINTED WITH OIL

Thou anointest my head with oil.
—Psalm 23:5b, KJV

E xodus 30:23-25 says, "Also take for yourself quality spices—five hundred shekels of liquid myrrh, half as much sweet-smelling cinnamon (two hundred and fifty shekels), and two hundred and fifty shekels of sweet-smelling cane, five hundred shekels of cassia, and a hin of olive oil: And you shall make from these a holy anointing oil, an ointment compounded according to the art of the perfumer. It shall be a holy anointing oil."

Oil was used in many different ways in the Old Testament. They would use it for cooking. They would use it as a repellent for insects, and, as we have seen with serpents, they would use it as a healing agent for cuts and deep wounds. The ingredients to make this holy compound came from trees, which is prophetic because Isaiah 61:3 says, "That they might be called the trees of righteousness, the planting of the Lord, that He may be glorified." This is referring to Jesus, the Tree of Life, and we, the trees of righteousness, the planting of the Lord. Note carefully that the anointing oil was specific in its use. It was used to anoint kings and priests and tabernacle articles. They would put it on the altar of incense, representing the people's prayers. The ingredients in the oil were precise in its compound. Let's take a deeper look at them.

FIVE HUNDRED SHEKELS OF MYRRH

The ingredient called myrrh is a sap-like resin that comes out of cuts in the bark of trees that are members of the Commiphora tree, commonly grown in the Arabian Peninsula, India, and northeastern Africa. Myrrh is a resin used for treating many things, including indigestion, ulcers, colds, cough, asthma, lung congestion, arthritis, pain, cancer, leprosy, and spasms. It is also used to stimulate and increase menstrual flow. Myrrh can be applied to the mouth for soreness and swelling, inflamed gums, gingivitis, loose teeth, and canker sores. It even cures bad breath. Myrrh can be used in foods as a flavor component and is also found in manufacturing as a compound to make fragrances, incense, and cosmetics. One of the primary uses in Old Testament times was for embalming dead bodies.

THE SPIRITUAL IMPLICATION

Myrrh is the bleeding of the tree, which denotes pain. Pain is an indicator that you are still alive, as my high school coach would say. I have come to know the God we served over the last thirty-three years that I have been a Christian, and I know that Romans 8:28 is so true when it says, "All things work together for good to those who love God, and to those who are called according to His purpose." I don't care how much pain you go through in life: God can and will use it for His purpose. No wonder He instructed the perfumer to put twice as much myrrh in the holy anointing oil. God will use your pain and use it to fuel your purpose and destiny.

TWO HUNDRED FIFTY SHEKELS OF CINNAMON

Cinnamon is the spice we have all come to love and use, whether in teas, candles, fragrances, chewing gum, or all sorts of foods. We love its smell. Moreover, we love the taste, whether in muffins, cinnamon rolls, or other baked delicacies. Cinnamon comes from inside the tree's bark, which is also suitable for essential oils, perfume, and flavoring. Cinnamon was also used to embalm bodies for burial.

THE SPIRITUAL IMPLICATION

This cinnamon spice speaks of life's good things that bring happiness and tranquility. It denotes the positive things happening in your life that bring you complete and utter joy, that propel you, and elevate you to a greater purpose. God will always take twice as much of your pain and mix it with the sweet things in your life that bring you joy and happiness. He knows how to work all things in your life to bring and produce power. A battery has a negative and a positive charge, making it powerful—so powerful it can crank your car motor to turn it on so you can go from one place to another. God uses the negative and the positive to produce power in you so you can go into all the world and be His instrument of righteousness to declare to all humanity that God is good.

TWO HUNDRED FIFTY SHEKELS OF CALAMUS

Calamus is a spice found in the root of a tree or bush whose resin is harvested for medicinal use to heal any infection. It was also a resin found in all sorts of perfume, and an ingredient for making gum. The resin became very popular with alcoholic drinks since it was a sweet spice. It was used in toothpaste, and since it was a sweet spice, bakers would use it for custards and rice pudding. The resin is a crucial ingredient to Dr Pepper: That's right, one of our favorite drinks has calamus in it.

THE SPIRITUAL IMPLICATION

We already understand that myrrh represents pain, and cinnamon represents the good things in life. Calamus represents our foundation—our root system, ethics, values, and belief systems. Calamus becomes the thing we build our life on; it's the why we do things and how we do things. It becomes the divine order that aligns us with God's purposes and will.

FIVE HUNDRED SHEKELS OF CASSIA

Cassia comes from the stems and heart of the bark of the cassia shrub or tree. The resin smells so much like the cinnamon tree many cannot tell the difference. Though the cassia tree has a much stronger scent than its cousin, the cinnamon tree, it is also an essential oil used for cooking and baking. Cassia would often replace cinnamon, but its powerful sweet fragrance was used primarily in hot oils and foods to promote a healthy immune system. During cold months cassia would defuse the cold with its warm, welcoming scent.

THE SPIRITUAL IMPLICATION

The fourth ingredient of the holy anointing oil is cassia, found in the tree's heart, which denotes our prayers, worship, hopes, and dreams. My friend, God takes our pain, a little of our good, and mixes them with a foundation of ethics and values that brings divine order into our lives as it is combined with a lot of prayer, worship, hopes, and dreams. He mingles all that with a hin of oil, and there you got the holy anointing oil that breaks yokes and removes burdens!

THE PURPOSE OF THE OIL

Isaiah 10:27 says, "It shall come to pass in that day that his burden will be taken away from your shoulder, and his yoke from your neck, and the yoke will be destroyed because of the anointing oil." The anointing breaks and destroys the yoke in our life that keeps us bound and oppressed. A yoke was a wooden crosspiece fastened over the necks of two animals and attached to the plow or cart they were to pull.

Jesus also used the yoke as a teaching or a doctrine. In Matthew 11:28-29 He says, "Come to Me, all you who labor and are heavy laden, and I will give you rest. Take My yoke upon you and learn from Me, for I am gentle and lowly in heart, and you will find rest for your souls." The yoke of the Mosaic Law was burdensome and heavy; it was hard to live out, but Jesus stood up and said to come to Him; His teaching and doctrine are easy, and the burden is light. Jesus taught a new teaching that ushered in the revelation of grace and truth.

OIL FOR THE SHEEP

In regards to the shepherd applying oil to the sheep, King David said "he anoints my head with oil." He understood the process; a shepherd would anoint every sheep with oil starting at the head because sheep could be competitive. Some would like to show off their dominance to everyone, and they would clash and bang their heads against one another, so the oil served as a protection for them.

Second, the shepherd would anoint the wool to eliminate flies, bugs, and fleas that would try to imbed in the sheep's skin, irritating it, and at times causing a skin infection. It was crucial to anoint the wool to eliminate this possibility. The third reason for the oil was to prevent flies and bugs from lodging in the sheep's nostrils and ears because, from time to time, the insects would lay eggs that would eventually travel to the sheep's brain. These larvae would then drive the sheep crazy, to the point where they would go around in a circle shaking their head, trying to loosen whatever had lodged there. It could get to the point where the sheep would find a rock or a hard place and bang their heads so hard that, if not caught in time, it would cause either brain damage or death.

THE SPIRITUAL IMPLICATION

According to Hebrews 6:2, part of the elementary principles of the foundations of Christ is the laying on of hands. We live in a day when we no longer see this expressed in our church services. We will have to return to the foundations of the principles of Christ, where we speak and experience the laying on of hands, as David refers to in Psalm 92:10 when he cries out to be anointed with fresh oil. The word *fresh* denotes green, which is symbolic of life. David is crying out for a fresh anointing of life that will give him the strength to persevere through life's struggles.

I also believe that it is imperative for shepherds to touch and anoint their sheep so that no false yokes (teachings, restrictions, or oppressions) can affect them in any way, shape, or form. This means calling them, speaking and praying, and even prophesying kind, encouraging words that get them out of their snare of thinking, so they can approach life with confidence and zest. We live in crucial times where we can't afford not to touch and teach and equip God's flock. So, let's take some anointing oil and start loving and anointing God's holy and beautiful sheep so that the spiritual bugs and flies, which are the demonic hosts, cannot oppress or suppress God's holy sheep.

CONCLUSION

As we have seen and understood the importance of the oil, we have discovered that all the ingredients come from within the tree. God takes a little bit of good, and a lot of your bad, and mixes that all in with some hopes and dreams, along with a lot of your prayer and worship, and mixes it in with a hin of oil. There you go, you have an anointing still in the business of breaking and destroying yokes and removing burdens far from God's holy people. Remember to allow this oil to flow to you and flow through you so that you become an extension of His glory!

CHAPTER 8
THE CUP OF REDEMPTION

My cup runneth over.
—Psalm 23:5, KJV

I n Bible times, they would always throw big festivals after harvest as a prophetic statement that God was good and very gracious to them in allowing them to prosper. It was a time to reflect on God's goodness during this time of great blessing.

When the children of Israel walked close to God, abiding by His covenant, they would prosper, in that the land would yield its crop because of the rain. When the children of Israel did not walk circumspectly upright before their God, the rain would not fall, causing them to be in famine. So, when they had a great harvest, they would all come together and celebrate the goodness of God. The king would invite his guests to join him at the banqueting table that was laid out with all kinds of lovely food and desserts. As it got later and later, you knew you were still welcome to stay at the king's table as his honored guest if he would personally fill your cup to overflowing. If this happened, it meant that the king was pleased with your presence and you could remain at the party. If he did not fill your cup to overflowing, that was his way of saying you were not welcome anymore.

So, you see, when King David writes in Psalm 23 of a cup running over, it means that the king is enjoying your company and you can remain as his guest, getting the royal treatment.

THE SILVER CUP OF REDEMPTION

Let's take a look at a familiar portion of scripture, the story of the life of Joseph, to explore this principle (see Genesis 41-46). Joseph had already interpreted the dreams that there would be seven years of plenty and seven years of famine. After being sold by his brothers, he eventually occupied a position of great authority in Egypt, second only to Pharaoh. The land had seven years of plenty and stored a certain amount of food in the storehouses. When the time of famine came, other nations began coming to Joseph for food year after year. The famine spread to Canaan, where Israel resided with his family. When his family came to him to buy food, Joseph recognized his brothers even though they did not recognize him. He told them not to come a second time unless they brought their little brother Benjamin.

As the famine continued and Israel, his sons, and their families were getting down to the last of their food, he asked his sons to return to Egypt and buy some more food. But they remembered what Joseph had said, that they would have to bring Benjamin with them. So after some deliberation, Israel decided to let Benjamin go. When Benjamin arrived and Joseph saw him, he immediately went to his chamber to weep because all the years of yearning for his little brother made him very emotional. After washing his face, Joseph said to serve his brothers bread so they might eat. As they loaded their donkeys with grain, Joseph told one of his men to put his silver cup (which in the Bible represents redemption) in Benjamin's grain bag. This shows us that Joseph was sharing the cup of redemption that he had already received, and when he purposed to reveal himself to his brothers, the empty cup would become a cup overflowing with blessings for his family.

Before it could become a cup that overflowed, however, Joseph had to reveal himself. He chose not to do so until his little brother

Benjamin appeared. Why? He was waiting until somebody came who looked just like him: Benjamin. The others were only half-brothers. Now Joseph could reveal himself and give the cup of redemption, where the price was paid in full. Jesus is our heavenly Joseph: He drank the cup in the Garden of Gethsemane, but He also filled that cup with an overflowing blessing.

There is a blessing that you don't have to work for. It's a blessing that belongs to you. It's not because you're good. It's because He is good! And because He is good, He has allowed you to be a part of the sheepfold of God. You have a good shepherd who is well-equipped and has paid the price for you and everybody who receives Him for salvation.

A WEALTHY PLACE

There is only one other place that is equivalent to "my cup runneth over," and that's in Psalm 66:12 (KJV), which reads, "Thou hast caused men to ride over our heads; we went through fire and through water: but thou broughtest us out into a wealthy place." The Hebrew word used for "wealthy place" and "my cup runneth over" is the same.

I get excited about Jesus and what He's done for us. In Luke 5, Peter and his fishing partners put out their nets, which changed their lives; their nets flowed over. Let's dig into what was going on. Jesus was walking along the shoreline with one foot in the water and one on land. Water is unstable and ground is stable. The Bible says He stood by the lake, or He stood in or above "the wealthy place." You see the lake they were fishing in was called Gennesaret.

Easton defines this place as a garden of riches. It was a wealthy place. Jesus has the ability to stand between stable and unstable because Jesus is God's Son and man's son. He is the hybrid of the ages that is not afraid of what is stable or unstable because He is God in the flesh. He wasn't just the son of man; He was the Son of God. He had God as His Father and Mary as His mother. His Father was from the realm of the supernatural and His mother was from the natural domain. He could (and can) walk in both spheres at the same time!

As the Father sent Jesus, so Jesus sends us. What was Jesus's job on earth? To bless. What is your job on earth? To bless—but you can only bless once you understand that He has made you a blessing. It's a cycle. God didn't make abundance for you to hoard. He made abundance for you to share. He healed you so you could have faith to lay your hands on others and bless them with healing. He prospered you financially so you could find a need and fill it. He gave you wisdom so you would walk in it and share it. He gave you relationships so you would grow and connect and learn how to out-give each other in those God-ordained relationships. The ultimate goal is that He makes you a blessing so that you become the blessing and the cup that overflows everywhere you go. He is a good, good shepherd desiring to be poured forth into His sheep, which are His people!

FISHING IN A WEALTHY PLACE

In Luke 5, they had been toiling all night and had caught no fish. When Jesus addressed Simon, He spoke to an unstable part of his nature. But Peter, the name he would become known by, means rock, and Simon means reed, denoting something easily shaken by the wind. Simon had gone fishing all night but caught nothing because he was unstable and double-minded. I am reminded of how James 1:6-8 says that "he who doubts is like a wave of the sea driven and tossed by the wind. For let not that man suppose that he will receive anything from the Lord; he is a double-minded man, unstable in all his ways." When Simon went out there was no blessing and nothing to show for his night of work. Jesus was not afraid of Simon's nothing because He understood who He was. He knew the Father had sent Him there to be a blessing, to be an extension of God's glory, and to be an extension of what the Father desired for Peter.

God wants you to understand that He is not afraid of your instability or situations that look hopeless or impossible. He's not scared of your disappointments, of those times when you feel like you're striving but have nothing to show for it. Because He is God, He will take you, like Simon Peter, to precisely where you caught "nothing," and He'll command you to go ahead and try again. Simon Peter threw the nets on the right side of the boat, and with Jesus on board, the results were very different! When Jesus tells you to revisit the place of nothingness, you won't return empty this time! He will make sure that your boat will overflow with blessing.

Jesus purchased our redemption. He drank the cup in the garden, but then He gave back that empty cup and said, "I have redeemed you all." You have not been redeemed with silver and gold but by the precious blood of Jesus Christ. His sacrifice and resurrection have brought you to a place where you can still hold that cup of redemption and live a life full of inheritance and blessing.

As a believer, you must now collect the spoils. The world must see the spoils, the goodness of God. They need to see it in your life and my life. We have been living too much in our discouraged places. We've been living too much in our disappointed places. I am here to tell you that those are enemies! And God has prepared a table right in the middle of every single one of those enemies, and He's not afraid of them. It is incredible that the word Gennesaret—which was where they were fishing—is called a garden of riches or a wealthy place. Jesus was trying to teach Peter a principal lesson, that it is impossible to catch nothing in a wealthy place. Jesus will always bring you back to where you've experienced disappointment and displeasure and cause things to turn in your favor simply because you are bone of His bone and flesh of His flesh. It is there that He makes known to you His phenomenal covenant so that you may at all times experience His wealthy place.

CONCLUSION

As we have journeyed along this great Psalm of reflection, we have come through valleys of the shadow of death to tables that have been prepared for us to feast at, and had our head anointed with the fresh oil of life. Coming to the overflowing cup that redeems and restores us to the prominent, promised place of our king, we move on toward His goodness and mercy that follow us all the days of our life.

CHAPTER 9

GOODNESS AND MERCY

Surely goodness and mercy shall follow me all the days of my life;
and I will dwell in the house of the Lord for ever.
—Psalm 23:6, KJV

I want to start this chapter with a story that will hopefully show you a glimpse of God's goodness. In 1989 I was a junior in college at Alaska Pacific University. I had been recruited to wrestle for the university, so my schedule was hectic like every athlete's. It consisted of a lot of study time at the library. Athletes always dreaded finals week because we would crash-study until three o'clock in the morning.

As I walked into my Anthropology class, everybody in the room was doing last-minute cramming. Then the professor entered and took a few minutes to review the subjects that were going to be on the test. Most of it was familiar, but there were some things that no one remembered ever hearing. The professor responded with what sent cold chills up our spines: "This is in your textbook, and you are responsible for learning it for the content of this exam." The time came for the test and he handed out every test facedown so that we could not see the front of the paper. Lo and behold, as we all began to turn the test over, we discovered that our professor had signed our names and filled out the test with all the correct answers. On top of my paper was an A+ and a handwritten note saying, "Joey, you were a pleasure to have in class. Thank you for your participation!" If only you could have been the to see everyone's faces as we all rejoiced. That was an incredible dose of goodness.

THE ELEVENTH-HOUR PEOPLE

Matthew 20:6-8 (KJV) says, "And about the eleventh hour he went out, and found others standing idle, and saith unto them, Why stand ye here all the day idle? They say unto him, Because no man hath hired us. He saith unto them, Go ye also into the vineyard; and whatsoever is right, that shall ye receive. So when even was come, the lord of the vineyard saith unto his steward, Call the labourers, and give them their hire, beginning from the last unto the first."

This parable that Jesus taught reveals the goodness of God. They all worked for the same amount of money: a denarius was the agreed wage. The eleventh-hour people received the same salary as those working all day. Of course, the people working all day didn't care that they worked longer, but they did agree to work for a denarius. The ones who only worked for one hour experienced the goodness of the vineyard landlord. The correlation between Jesus's parable and my university experience is very similar. My whole class experienced the goodness of our professor by him taking the test for all of us after we had been studying all night. And the eleventh-hour people experienced the goodness of the vineyard landlord after just working an hour and getting paid for the whole day. The goodness of God is like that—getting something you did not expect, let alone deserve, and being surprised, exceedingly and abundantly above anything you could ask, think, or imagine.

THE GOODNESS OF GOD DEFINED

We often sing about the goodness of God or repeat our little religious cliches, like when the preacher says, "God is good . . . " The congregation replies, "All the time!" He shouts back, "And all the time . . . " and the congregation responds, "God is good!"

The Bible defines God's goodness in two ways. One has to do with His character, and the other one focuses on His actions. Psalm 119:68 (NLT) says it best: "You are good and do only good." The first half of that verse focuses on the fact that God is, by nature, good. He is morally excellent, beautiful, and extravagantly bountiful. God is the original definition of good! This is what Jesus meant in Mark 10:18 when He said, "No one is good but One," and that is God. The second definition of God's goodness concentrates on what God does. This is what makes God holy, the fact that everything He is, says, and does is congruent. God reveals His goodness—which is His God-ness—through avenues of kindness.

Another way God shows His goodness is through His generosity and His steadfast love and grace. I love what Jeremiah 29:11 (NLT) says, ". . . 'I know the plans I have for you,' says the LORD. 'They are plans for good and not for disaster, to give you a future and a hope.'" God's plans for every one of His sheep are filled with His goodness. You become the object of His affection, and because of God's divine nature, everything that He expresses toward you comes from the overwhelming, overflowing, gargantuan God-size heart of His goodness.

In Psalm 23:6, King David is trying to let the reader know that the pathway of the just shines brighter and brighter regardless of your present situation. He is reassuring you that, from God's perspective, He will work all things for your good, even if you experience some uncomfortable turbulence in your life journey. Hopefully, you will have a better glimpse of the goodness of God and His extravagant love for you. As surely as His goodness follows you all the days of your life, so does His extravagant mercy. Let's take a deeper look at the mercy of God.

THE MERCY OF GOD

The mercy of God is broad, and we could teach this subject for a year. But to simplify the word, it simply means compassion and forgiveness. This is very crucial, because most Christians do not have a good grip on the mercy of God. To understand it better we must, without a shadow of a doubt, understand the cross at Calvary. The cross ushered in the mercy of God in that the cross was where Jesus shed His blood for all of humanity. The blood of Jesus Christ was the price for your forgiveness or your mercy; Jesus's blood made you in right standing with God almighty and gave you an identity of sonship and kingship. I'm reminded of Genesis 4:10, where God speaks to Cain and says, "What have you done? The voice of your brother's blood cries out to Me from the ground." The voice of Abel cried out "vengeance," while the blood of Jesus has been crying out "mercy" until now.

Lamentations 3:22-23 (KJV) states, "It is of the Lord's mercies that we are not consumed, because his compassions fail not. They are new every morning: great is thy faithfulness." My friend, did you catch that? The mercies of God are new every morning. That means today, when you got up, forgiveness was staring you in the face. Tomorrow when you get up, His mercies will wait until you get moving, and guess what? That's right, they will start following you. The word for *follow* in Hebrew denotes running after or chasing you like a dog. The mercies of God are chasing me and you down like a dog, except they do not want to devour us; they want to bless us with compassion and forgiveness. Jesus's death provided His extravagant mercies to be our portion so we would be without reason for coming into His presence and fullness. Know one thing, that tomorrow when you get up, His goodness and His mercy will follow you and chase you down all the days of your life.

DWELLING IN THE HOUSE OF THE LORD

Psalm 92:13-15 (KJV) says it best: "Those that be planted in the house of the Lord shall flourish in the courts of our God. They shall still bring forth fruit in old age; they shall be fat and flourishing." The word for *flourish* is the Hebrew one that means to bloom, to break out, to grow, and *Strong's Concordance*'s definition renders the word to fly. When you get rooted, it's only then you will get fruit! A blessing comes from being rooted in the house of the Lord. You will have the strength and energy to have kids in your old age, and you will be fat and flourishing (laugh out loud!). The word for fat in the Hebrew denotes being wealthy, and the word flourishing here is different than the other word flourish in the previous verse. *Flourishing* denotes fresh, full of life, and new. That means the blessing of being planted in the house of the Lord revives me, refreshes me, and replenishes me to overcome in life.

THE HOUSE OF OBED-EDOM

2 Samuel 6:11 (NKJV) says, "The ark of the LORD remained in the house of Obed-Edom the Gittite three months. And the LORD blessed Obed-Edom and all his household." In the Old Testament,

the Tabernacle that Moses erected was the house of God, and He somehow lived in between the faces of the cherubim in the most holy place called the Ark of the Covenant. Anytime God commanded Israel to move, the Levites had to pack up the church and move with God's presence. The children of Israel became so known throughout all the land because of this box they carried which held the presence of God. It provoked much envy from the Philistines, who wanted the box because they knew there was something about it.

After capturing the box, the Philistines find out very quickly that a blessing for the children of Israel can, in a heartbeat, become a curse to someone who is not in covenant with God. Suddenly, great chaos emerges in the Philistine camp; the god they serve falls and crumbles to pieces, and everybody has a bad case of hemorrhoids. When David is anointed king, he goes against the Philistines and destroys them, along with the Jebusites, to recover what is now known as the City of David. In trying to retrieve the ark of the covenant, David runs into a hiccup on the road that causes a young man by the name of Uzzah to try to steady the ark when they hit a breach in the road. Uzzah dies that day! And so David leaves the ark in Obed-Edom's house, which is the beginning of Obed-Edom's obsession with it. Everything in Obed-Edom's life starts to flourish. His tomato plants grow to twice the usual size. His cattle start to have triplets. He experiences a bumper harvest. Things just prosper for Obed-Edom's house simply because the house of God is present.

When David figures out how to successfully move the ark, guess who is there when it is time to sing or play an instrument? That's right, Obed-Edom. Guess who signs up when they are looking for doorkeepers to guard the ark? Yep, Obed-Edom. He has been so extravagantly blessed that all he ever wants to do is be near that ark. I think King David knew a little bit of that when he said that "surely goodness and mercy shall follow me all the days of my life: and I will dwell in the house of the Lord forever." David had a great understanding of how much God loved him and his people. No matter what! God's goodness and mercy remain the same.

CONCLUSION

We have just learned about God's goodness and mercy and the importance of being planted in the house of God. I hope you have been challenged, charged, and inspired to receive His extravagant goodness and the overwhelming overflow of His mercy. Remember, they are new every morning! And I hope you get a hunger for being planted in a local church through having read this. In more than three decades of being a Christian, I have discovered that my life is much better being planted in the house of God, where I know I will be guarded and guided. So, let's find roots in the old church house and see the prosperity of our God.

LAST THOUGHTS

God wants to take us on a journey, and Psalm 23 gives us a beautiful picture of that process. We have a good shepherd who causes us not to want and makes us lie down in abundance in the pastures of green goodness. He then leads us beside still waters where we can drink in His presence and thirst no more. He navigates through our impossible situations with one foot in the water and one foot on the land. He restores our souls, leading us on the path of righteousness. And, even when we walk through the valley of the shadow of death, He is with us, and we do not have to fear. His rod and staff keep us in order on the straight and narrow and protect us. He is so good that He prepares a table in the presence of our enemies. He cares for us when we're in our tight places. He cares that we make it through. Then He anoints our head with oil and causes our cup to run over with an abundance of honor.

May you have the faith and the illumination to recognize now that He is the great and Chief Shepherd of all shepherds, the King of all kings. He takes care of His own! Living by faith isn't easy, but God has your back. He is your sustainer. He is your protector, and He looks out for your welfare. Let Him protect you and show you a life filled with blessings. God is the Good Shepherd!

CPSIA information can be obtained
at www.ICGtesting.com
Printed in the USA
JSHW011151250523
42234JS00006B/23

9 781960 678256